THE PHILIPPINES
Rediscovered

E.B. EDDY PAPER
Luna Gloss 100lb. Text

THE PHILIPPINES
Rediscovered

Photography by Stuart Naval Dee

Book Project Director: Dann Ilicic, Big Eye Creative
Designer: Iain Hamilton, Big Eye Creative
Design Consultant: Andy Naval
Editorial Consultant: Elizabeth V. Reyes

Printed and bound in Canada
Printed on 100lb Luna Gloss from E.B. Eddy Paper

This book was made possible through the generous assistance and sponsorship of the
Philippine Department of Tourism.

Canadian Cataloguing in Publication Data

Dee, Stuart.
 The Philippines rediscovered

 ISBN 0-9684027-0-4 (bound) — ISBN 0-9684927-1-2 (pbk.)

 1. Philippines—Pictorial works. I. Title.
DS656.2.D43 1998   959.904'8'0222   C98-910885-6

To Mom and Dad, for all your love through the years,

and for giving us the best of the cultures of the East and West

&

To all Filipinos

Foreword

THE PHILIPPINES is perhaps best known for the banner headline events that highlight our country's recent history. You probably saw the dramatic television coverage of People Power and our return to democracy. The powerful eruption of Mount Pinatubo was front page copy in most dailies. It also was not too long ago that the financial pages were trumpeting the painstaking revival of our economy. Unfortunately, that was prior to the now-raging Asian contagion grabbing the headlines.

But there is a much more compelling story to tell. A tale composed of many small vignettes that collectively define us as a nation. Here we find the countless triumphs of the human spirit despite the bittersweet reality of everyday life. Here too lies the resilient and magnificent beauty of mother nature. And perhaps here too we may glimpse the subtle hand of God.

Stuart Dee's *The Philippines Rediscovered* thoughtfully explores this woven fabric of our nation. May you find in its pages the essence of what will continue to define our nation long after recent events become distant memory.

Corazon C. Aquino
Former President of the Philippines

Introduction

To Remember and to Sing in Photographs

FOR THE CENTENNIAL celebrations, Filipino as well as foreign photographers had a literal field day for shoots that were more than documentation. Thousands of pictures—black and white and full-color—of Philippine culture and history were taken, hundreds of them to become the better part of those Centennial coffee-table books. More than Centennial, *The Philippines Rediscovered* is timeless.

Stuart Dee y Naval is not just an ordinary photographer, as this book of his photographs so stunningly proves. Born in the Philippines, he migrated to Canada and studied fine arts and photography. Now, based in Vancouver, he pays his native land the tribute: *to remember and to sing in photographs*.

To Filipino eyes, some of the scenes Stuart captures with his camera may be familiar, but in a manner that is at once so distinctive one would wish to see them again, feel them, even live with and in them. This is the essence of a loving remembrance akin to an anthem in the heart.

A creatively imaged picture matters much as art only when the subject of the eyes behind the lens finds a depth of kinship in the final viewer's rediscovery. Thus, with this book, Stuart Dee gives us special views that rediscover for us the Philippines, each one beautiful in its own light and life, and collectively even more so in their becoming a living moment of that vocation which is ours—*to remember and to sing*.

Nick Joaquin
National Artist

From the Photographer

HAVING THE GOOD fortune of travelling to distant lands and experiencing different cultures through my vocation, a desire to visit and photograph my homeland grew over the years. I wanted to see the country of my childhood, to rediscover what I had seen before, and to discover what I had never seen.

Finally, in 1994, two decades after my family had left the Philippines, I went back to start recording my impressions. Over the following five years, I returned many times. The odyssey was long and arduous—sometimes even painful—but it was most rewarding. I saw more of the islands than most people would in a lifetime. By spending time photographing in the country, talking to and living with Filipinos, I not only recorded fragments of their lives and learned so much about the culture, I also rediscovered myself. I now better understand why I think, feel and act the way I do.

This book is not a travel guide or a visual cross-section of the Philippines. The intention was to capture and share her beauty, like how one might try to photograph a dear friend, and to include some 'candid' shots to show other facets of her character and her life story.

Whether foreigner or Filipino, I hope the images here reveal some aspects of the country unknown to you and inspire you to discover this beautiful land in person.

My sincerest thanks to all whose words, support, and friendship made this challenging journey not only possible, but also enlightening.

Stuart N. Dee
Vancouver, Canada

…on the way to Balicasag, I saw a tiny island with a few coconut trees—it seemed like the quintessential desert island paradise. The next day, I asked around and found a fisherman who would take me there. I noticed the damp interior of the banca, *and asked about leaks, for the safety of my camera equipment. 'No problem,' he said, 'no leaks.' As he dragged his boat to the water's edge, he remarked that he forgot something very important, and said he'd be right back… I thought he was getting some gas for his small motor, but he came back with a bottle of liquor… as he paddled out, water started seeping quickly into the* banca… *as I turned around to bring it to his attention, he was already nonchalantly bailing the water out…*

Above: Dawn at Lubuagan,
Kalinga-Apayao.

Opposite: The rice terraces in northern
Luzon are the most extensive in the
world and have been declared a UNESCO
World Heritage Site. Built by hand over
two thousand years ago, they would
extend for over 20,000 kilometers
if joined end to end.

They told me that even elderly ambassadors who want to see it make the hike with no problems, so I was confident I could do it with ease. I was dead wrong. Halfway to Batad, at the top of the highest ridge, we rested and discussed the merits of continuing on. Susan, who I thought might give up, was ready to go on. Felix, who was puffing cigarettes on the way up, and who I was sure would give up, was also determined. The pain in my knees voted to turn back. Then Chris, the English kid, showed up... he had hiked an extra few kilometers than we had, from Banaue to the start of the trail at Bangaan, to the ridge, carrying a fifty-pound backpack. I had to go on... we finally made it... the beautiful sight made it all worthwhile, but we had to hike back before nightfall... we took a longer route with a more gradual slope, to ease the excruciating pain in my knees... there was an unattended soft-drink stand, it had a price list and an open container for the money... one of those heartwarming little things that puts one's faith back in humanity... towards the end, the sound of crickets and running streams, together with the fireflies darting about, made it a magical hike back and made the pain bearable...

Opposite: A two-hour hike from Bangaan, Batad has the most impressive terraced amphitheater. There are no roads, so everything, from construction materials to food, has to be brought to the village by foot.

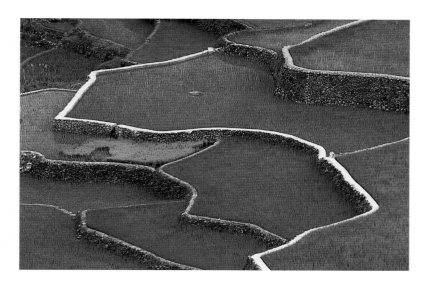

Each region's terraces have a different character. *Top:* Hapao; *Center:* Sagada; *Bottom:* Banaue.

Opposite: Using an ingenious system of natural springs, holes and dikes, the proper water level at each terrace is controlled and maintained.

The Philippine beast of burden, the carabao, is the farmer's best friend.

Left: Taking a mud bath to cool off.

Laundry day in northern Luzon.

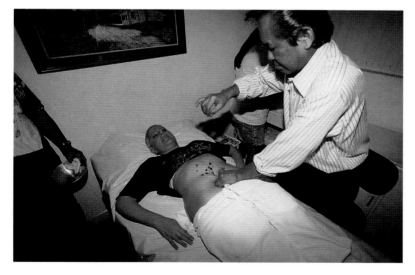

Above: A local 'ambulance' rushes a pregnant woman to the hospital. Kalinga-Apayao.

Left: Thousands from around the globe visit faith healers, mostly in Baguio, seeking miracle cures.

A half-buried chapel façade symbolizes the massive devastation of the Mt. Pinatubo eruption in 1991. Pampanga.

We were driving around Pampanga to view the aftermath of the eruptions… the lahar-covered monochrome landscape could've been from another planet, everything looked bleak… then, in the distance, I noticed some people with golf clubs… we stopped to check it out… the locals had created 'Poor Man's Golf Course' out of the abundant lahar. The greens were definitely a bit fast, but the course was complete with a clubhouse, with trophies and tournament charts… as always, they had improvised and made the best of what was given…

Some edible lilies grow amid the fish
pens in Lake Sebu, South Cotabato.

Fish drying, El Nido town.

Fish is a staple throughout the islands. Fresh catch in Cagayan de
Oro, El Nido, and Puerto Princesa...

Selling yarn in Banaue, salted eggs and chili in Legaspi, Albay. The labuyo chili is said to be the hottest pepper and is widely used in the local Bicol cuisine.

The islands are dotted with falls. Bomod-ok Falls in Sagada, and Katibawasan Falls in Camiguin.

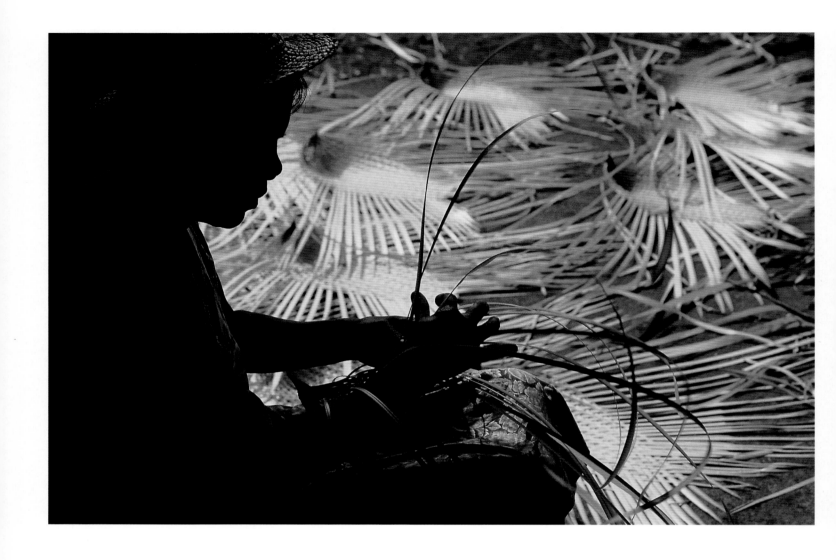

After studying the intricacy of a fan, I asked one of the ladies there if she could show me a sample of how it's done. Assuming each fan was made from many different parts and trying to guess how many hours it would take, she astounded me by whipping one up in a few minutes, with incredible speed and dexterity, from a single palm leaf...

Left: Baskets in Antiquera.

Below: Native crafts and souvenirs for sale, Baguio.

Vigan in Ilocos Sur has some of the most
well-preserved Spanish colonial houses,
built by wealthy Chinese merchants.
The *kalesa*, a two-wheeled horse-drawn
carriage, is still widely used around town.

Stables in Subic Bay offer horseback rides
through the forests.

The *terno* is the modern version of the traditional Filipina dress.

T'boli men, Lake Sebu, South Cotabato.

...three older men were in conversation. I hesitated bringing the camera to my eye in case it might distract them. After a few minutes, I did. They noticed me but it did not change their behavior one bit. In other parts of the country, a lot of the people either shy away or shout 'take my picture, take my picture!' The T'boli seem to have a certain quiet dignity, and they just went about their regular business without being affected by the 'visitor.'

Above: A bronze monument in Palo, Leyte immortalizes General Douglas MacArthur's 1944 landing and fulfillment of his promise 'I shall return!' His return began the liberation of the Philippines and the end of WWII.

Right: The skeletal remnants of barracks in Corregidor remain as monuments to the heroic Filipino and American soldiers that defended the islands.

National Hero Jose Rizal's monument in Luneta Park marks the exact spot
where he became a martyr for his country. A brilliant Renaissance man,
his writings and his execution ultimately led to Philippine independence
from Spain.

Manila, the political, financial
and cultural center, is home to
11 million people.

Opposite: EDSA , the site of the peaceful
1986 People Power revolution that
toppled a dictatorship and restored
democracy to the nation.

Above : Makati, the business district.

Left: Roxas Boulevard and Manila Bay.

A merchant minds his shop in Chinatown.

The MacArthur Suite was rebuilt in honor of the general, who stayed
at the Manila Hotel and used it as headquarters during the war.

Opposite: A symbol of the Philippines and Philippine ingenuity, the first jeepneys were created by Filipinos from surplus army jeeps at the end of WWII. They are still widely used for public transport and seen all over the islands. The classic hand-painted jeepneys are fast disappearing; the current models usually have bright neon stick-on decorations.

Below: A local policeman on 'official duty' in Tagbilaran. The siesta is another holdover from the Spanish.

Old and New Manila:

Right: Casa Manila.

Below: The Baluerte de San Diego in Intramuros, the old walled city.

Opposite: Grand Lobby of the Shangri-La Hotel, Makati.

Visitors and locals enjoy the much-touted
Manila Bay Sunset.

Manila is also known for its varied and
vibrant nightlife.

Local and foreign polo teams play matches every weekend during the dry season at the Manila Polo Club.

The *kalesa* can still be seen in Manila's
Chinatown and other parts of the country.

Opposite: A former mayor painted the ceiling of Panglao Church.

Above: A boy makes an offering at the Taoist Temple in Cebu.

Left: The Gothic-Renaissance Molo Church in Iloilo.

Above: Tomatoes, Ilocos Norte.

Right: The *kamias* is a sour fruit used in *sinigang*, a native soup dish with seafood, or pork, or beef, mixed with a variety of vegetables.

My friend's father insisted that I look at his kamias tree in the back. The moment I saw the mass of tiny, sour green fruit hanging off the trunk, it instantly brought me back almost a quarter century, to the days my brothers, my cousins and I would play around the kamias tree in the back yard... we'd use slingshots to strike down santol and kaymito fruit from the trees beside it... I hadn't seen this tart fruit in years, yet the mere sight of it caused me to salivate...

66

Fruitstands line the roads of Cavite on
the way to Tagaytay Ridge from Manila.

St. James in Alabang is one of the more modern churches.

Paoay Church in Ilocos Norte has Javanese, Chinese and
Spanish influences. Created in 'Earthquake Baroque' style with
heavy buttresses, its thick walls are made of coral limestone,
plastered brick and mortar mixed with sugar cane juice.

Above: The twin spires of the Cathedral in Puerto Princesa tower over houses on the water.

Right: The Protestant *Iglesia ni Kristo* churches exhibit the same architectural style throughout the islands.

The mosque at Taluksangay.
Most of the country's four million
Muslims live in Mindanao.

Every morning, thousands of tuna, some of them weighing over a hundred kilos, are landed manually on the beach in General Santos City. The fish are weighed right on the beach, where Japanese and local buyers bid on them.

Right: Fish, blood and Christ.

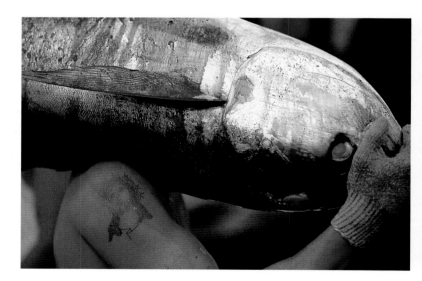

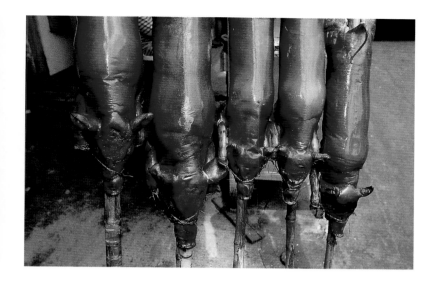

Lechon, or roast suckling pig, is standard fare for fiestas and other special gatherings or celebrations.

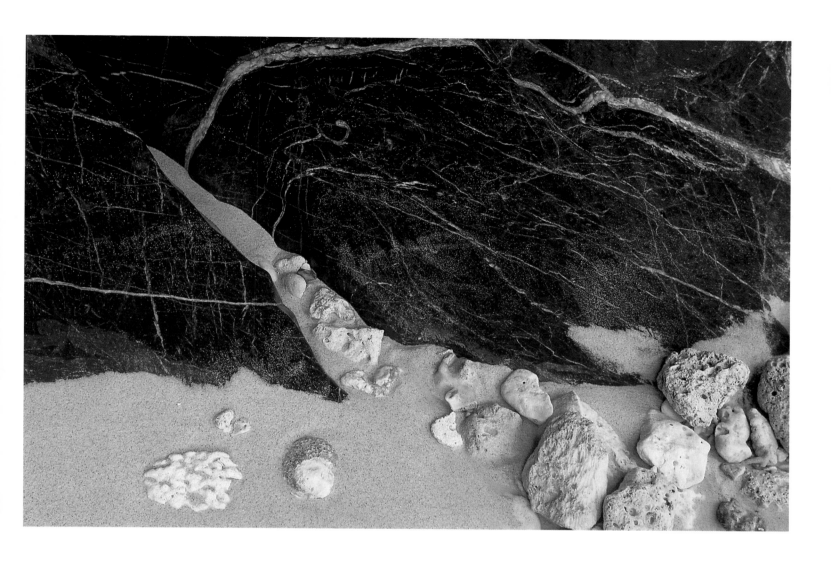

A fisherman's simple lunch may consist
of rice, a mango, and his catch.
El Nido, Palawan.

Above: A practice influenced by the Chinese custom of having noodles to wish a long life for the birthday celebrant, spaghetti is a tradition at children's birthday parties. Boracay.

Left: Native hot dog stand, Kalibo.

Cebu City, the oldest in the country, is the second largest metropolis.

Opposite: Some faithful light votive candles for special prayers or thanks in the Basilica Minore del Santo Niño. A replica of Magellan's cross, containing a relic of the original cross he planted on landing in 1521, is housed nearby.

Below: Fuente Osmeña Circle is the landmark in the heart of the city.

Rosaries, Santo Niño figures, and other religious articles are sold just outside the basilica.

On the strange confluence of conservative Spanish traditions and more liberal American attitudes imparted during their respective administrations, it is said that 'Filipinos went through 300 years in a convent and 50 years in Hollywood.' A religious calendar and cheesecake calendar coexist, without contradiction, at a security guard's post.

Opposite: A young girl's first holy communion. Daraga.

Above: Many faithful make a pilgrimage to the Lourdes Grotto in Baguio during Holy Week.

Left: Young girls make rosaries as part of a social program.

Despite some opposition, cockfighting remains a local institution.
Cockfights happen every Sunday in most towns and cities.

Right: Digital cash register used by a street vendor.

… even more interesting to watch are the incredible kristos—amid the frenzied crowds and noise, they take and confirm the bets through hand signals, memorizing scores of bets at different odds with different people. After each fight, a flurry of rolled paper money is tossed back and forth and all bets are settled. All this without a thing being written, with no errors, no arguments… I still find it hard to believe, even after seeing it…

Previous pages and this page: In honor of the patron saint of farmers, St. Isidore, the town of Lucban celebrates the Pahiyas Festival every May 15th, as an offering for a good harvest. Colorful rice wafers are used to decorate the whole town; afterwards, they can be eaten as a snack.

The San Agustin Church and Manila Cathedral have a wedding every hour on the hour on busy Saturdays. Some of the more extravagant receptions have thousands of guests.

To maximize available resources, the jeepney is often overloaded.

Left: Each region has a unique weave pattern on the façades of the homes.

Shortly after setting up a tripod to shoot a bicycle against a colorful façade, dozens of students started crowding around to watch. Taking some time to make varying compositions of the scene with different lenses, I noticed a young boy that seemed particularly engrossed. Halfway through the shoot, he finally asked the guide something in Visayan, the local dialect. I asked what he wanted to know. He was asking why I am taking so many pictures of this old rusting bike, when there are so many newer ones around the corner...

Boracay, an island off Aklan, has miles of
white, flour-fine sand and is a favorite
among tourists and locals.

Above: Calamansi, a tiny citrus fruit, is used for the local version of lemonade. Banaue.

Quiapo market has everything from
produce to handicrafts to live chickens
to magic potions.

The Philippine archipelago boasts the widest variety of marine life, with over 2000 species of fish alone. This diversity, combined with exceptional visibility, make dive spots in Bohol, Batangas, Palawan and Cebu popular with divers from around the world.

Shooting the rapids in Pagsanjan Falls, Laguna. Boatmen pull visitors upstream in dugout *bancas* and guide them through rocks and boulders during the thrilling, wet ride downstream.

Watermelon stands line the river by the university in Iloilo, where students and other locals relax and feast on the succulent fruit.

Cebu's major fiesta, the Sinulog Festival, is a weeklong celebration that includes dancing, fireworks and a procession through the streets.

The Ati-atihan festival in Kalibo is a three-day, carnival-like fiesta with a powerful beat that compels everyone to join the dancing in the streets.

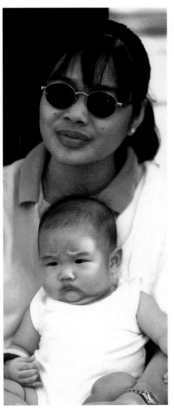

As we finally entered the Big Lagoon, the boatman shut off the motor... there wasn't another soul around... the combination of utter stillness and stunning beauty was powerful. I knew then that no matter what I did, I could never capture this on film... as eager as I was to record the beauty, I had to simply stare and take it all in for a few minutes... I had the strangest feeling that I had to come back to this place, when I hadn't even left it...

El Nido, a marine paradise, has limestone cliffs, bat caves, secret lagoons, exotic vegetation and crystal clear waters.

Above: A nipa hut in Pinagbuyutan Island.

Left: A natural bonsai in Shimizu Island.

Lake Taal is in fact the crater of an older, extinct volcano. The modern Taal Volcano sits in the center, and its own crater lake has another island. Thus, it's an island in a lake in an island in a lake in an island in the sea.

Local legend explains the hundreds of mysterious haycock hills around Carmen, Bohol as the hardened tears of a giant whose love was unrequited. They are called the Chocolate Hills due to their brown hue in the summer.

Above: Filipinas are known for their natural grace and warmth.

Right: Davao is one of the orchid-growing centers.

Opposite: Shell ladies sell seashells by the seashore in Balicasag Island. The Philippine archipelago has one of the greatest variety of shells, with over 21,000 different species—more than a fifth of all known species.

Beauty pageants continue to be popular, and many Filipinas go on to win international pageants.

Opposite: Filipino food is said to be best eaten the traditional way, with bare hands, served on banana leaves.

Right: A vendor sells her produce on a footbridge in Rio Hondo.

Villa Escudero in Laguna offers visitors a most authentic Filipino-style picnic. A few inches of cool running water on the ground makes the whole experience extremely refreshing.

Left: Hidden Valley, also in Laguna, has hot and cold springs, a gorge, and a waterfall.

The country has one of the highest literacy rates in Asia, due in large part to the extensive school system.

Above: The tricycle is another popular mode of transport throughout the islands.

Left: A *taho* (a snack made of bean curd) vendor brings home the chicken by jeepney.

The number of skulls attached to the side of an Ifugao house designate status and wealth—this particular one has dozens on all four sides. Banaue.

The Aetas trained the US Army in jungle warfare, teaching them survival techniques. Now, they entertain and educate the tourists. I've seen the lowly, simple bamboo used in different ways and to make different things, from utensils, rafts, furniture, to houses, but the demos revealed their mastery and creativity… they showed how to get pure water… how to make not just a cooking vessel, but an automatic rice cooker with a built-in lid, lid holder and lock,… to make fire, they don't just rub sticks together, they make six different parts of the fire-maker with which they can make fire within seconds…

Previous pages: Yakan woven cloths are known for their fine weave and bright colors. Zamboanga.

Nipa, the palm used for huts, grows on the banks of the Loboc River in Bohol.

Visitors enter the St. Paul's Subterranean River and view the strange rock formations and resident bats. Palawan.

Opposite: Thousands of bats hang out on trees till feeding time at dusk. Subic Bay, Zambales.

Above: With a wingspan of more than two meters, the Philippine eagle is the largest in the world. This endangered species has been bred successfully in captivity at the Davao Eagle Center.

Right: A monitor lizard's foot- and tail-prints, Palawan.

Above: Vintas with their colorful sails, Zamboanga.

Left: A sea cucumber gatherer, Camiguin.

143

Opposite: A *tuba* (palm wine) gatherer climbs a tree twice a day to collect the sap from the flower in the crown of a coconut palm. Davao.

Above: A fisherman tends to his fish pens, Taal Lake.

Looking more like a housing subdivision, the Chinese Cemetery
has mausoleums—some towering up to three stories high—with
bedrooms, bathrooms, kitchens and even mailboxes.

Camiguin, an island off Mindanao, boasts volcanoes, waterfalls, virgin forests, hot and cold springs, and a white-sand island simply called White Island.

A showcase of Filipino ingenuity, craftsmanship and creativity, the Plantation Bay Resort in Cebu is the only five-star resort in Asia completely created and built by an all-Filipino team of architects, designers, engineers and technicians.

Filipinos are well-known for their dancing and singing talents.
The Singkil dance has strong Muslim influences.

Dancers in native dress, Kalinga-Apayao.

The Saturday Group of artists draw and
paint a figure in one of their weekly sessions.

Right: Cebu is the guitar-making capital.

Below: Kiln and pottery-making in Alburquerque, Bohol.

The town of Paete is named after the woodcarvers' tool, the *paet*, or chisel. Skilled craftsmen carve everything from the Last Supper to Hollywood icons for the local and world-wide market.

Watching them at work, the talent and versatility these humble carvers mastered through the generations become apparent. They carve everything from chess pieces to full-sized figures, including cigar-store Indians that you see in the States... some of the discarded, half-finished works were the most beautiful—they reminded me of Michelangelo's unfinished sculptures breaking free and releasing themselves from the medium...

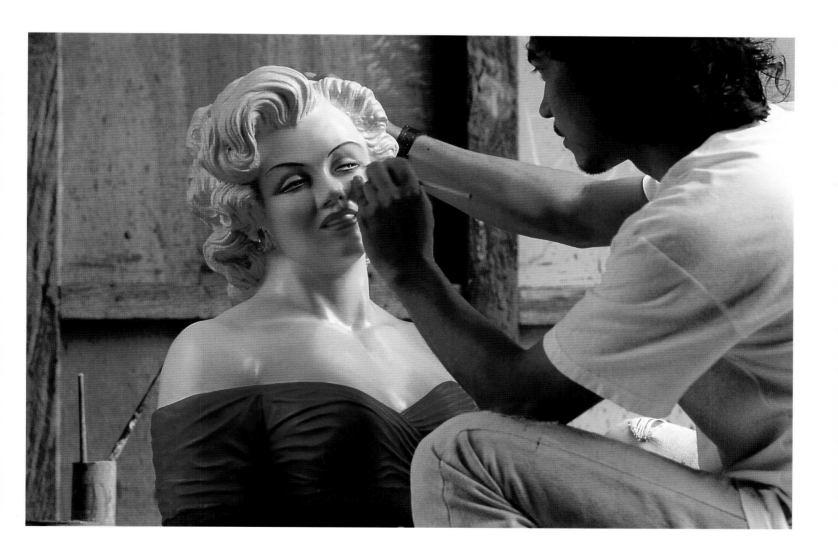

Muslims at the mosque and at the market.

Opposite: Fish vendor, Taluksangay.

Native houses on stilts, Samal Island.

The Miniloc Resort cottages, El Nido.

Opposite: A young boy gets a manual shower alfresco.

Left: Sipa is an indigenous game where players take turns kicking the ball into the air, cracking a 'whip' with each hit. Teams are scored on the basis of their gracefulness, the sound of the whip, and how long they can keep the ball in the air.

Below: Basketball is the country's most popular sport. One finds makeshift courts all over the islands, including simple hoops attached to coconut trees.

Previous pages: *I visited the Samal people living in houses on stilts. You'd think they would have only the bare necessities of a simple life, but they had TV's, kareoke machines and pool tables!... the kids were so excited about someone photographing them, they were all scampering about and jumping from plank to plank, following me and my assistant... a few seconds after I stepped back into the boat, the plank carrying all the curious kids collapsed and they all fell into the water... they resurfaced laughing and climbed back up...*

Left: Measuring only about five inches, the carnivorous tarsier is the smallest primate in the world and is most commonly found in the island of Bohol.

Previous pages: Considered to have a perfect cone shape, Mayon Volcano's last major eruption was in 1814, covering the whole town of Cagsawa with lava—only the church belfry remains today. Albay.

Eid El Fitr celebrates the end of the fast of Ramadan. Muslim women and young children are segregated from the men as they worship at the King Faisal Mosque in Marawi.

Above: An El Shaddai gathering in Luneta Park attracts tens of thousands of followers.

Left: Outdoor mass at the basilica in Cebu City.

Opposite: Bukidnon has some of the
largest pineapple plantations in the world.

Above: Curacha, a cousin of the crab
and the lobster, is the seafood specialty
in Zamboanga.

177

Filipinos have the longest Christmas season in the world. Yuletide carols start playing in October and the lights are up till February. In Tanjay, it is literally Christmas *every* single day of the year. The Christmas lights and decorations on the City Hall building, a giant tree, and the streets are never taken down.

We had a hectic day of island-hopping and shooting since sunrise, and I was looking forward to having dinner at the Stargazer, the outdoor

dining area. The guests were marveling at the millions of stars and the Hale-Bopp comet, clearly visible at the time… a cool breeze

made the it one of those perfect evenings… I was wondering about the cosmos, and if life existed elsewhere in the universe… the guests

at the next table were trying to spot and name constellations… finally, one says 'I don't get how they get all those figures from the stars,

I mean, how do you get a half-man, half-horse archer with a bow and arrow from a few stars? Why not a monkey playing a fiddle?'

I hardly ever see this kind of warmth openly displayed in other countries... seeing their affectionate nature is so heartwarming it moves me... it reminds me that as kids, we were like that, putting arms around each other... it was the most natural thing to do... why should it be 'unnatural' now—can one ever go back?... ... ... is this my Ithaca ... is Penelope here?

We finally reached the desert island… I met a group of fishermen… they asked me to join them for lunch. Even with their modest means and simple ways, the genuine Filipino hospitality shows through. They started cleaning out their catch, and I wondered how they were going to cook it—there wasn't a hibachi for miles… they simply barbecued the fish and squid on a coconut husk and served it on a wooden oar… it was the humblest of meals, yet it was the most memorable…

… over time, what becomes apparent is the underlying happiness… no matter what their circumstances, they seem really happy… one may have more material wealth than most of them, but they have truer wealth… paradise is truly found within…

N

W   E

S

0   50   100   150   200

KILOMETRES

SABTANG ISLAND

BATAN ISLAND

BABUYAN ISLAND

BABUYAN
ISLANDS

LAOAG   APARRI

VIGAN   TUGUEGARAO

SAGADA
BONTOC
BANAUE

SAN FERNANDO

BAGUIO

THE

PHILIPPINES

ALAMINOS
LINGAYEN   **DAGUPAN**

SANTA CRUZ   LUZON

TARLAC

ANGELES

OLONGAPO   SAN FERNANDO

SUBIC BAY   **MANILA**

QUEZON CITY

CAVITE

PHILIPPINE
SEA

NASUGBU   LUCBAN   DAET

LUCENA
BATANGAS   CATANDUANES I.

PUERTO GALERA   MARINDUQUE I.

SOUTH

CHINA

SEA

MINDORO   SIBUYAN
SEA

LEGASPI

SORSOGON

ROXAS

BUSUANGA ISLAND

CULION I.   CORON I.

LINAPACAN I.

EL NIDO

TAYTAY

ROXAS

BORACAY I.

KALIBO

ROXAS

PANAY

CADIZ

ILOILO

BACOLOD

GUIMARAS I.

PANAY GULF

MASBATE

MASBATE

SAMAR

VISAYAN

ISLANDS

CEBU   LEYTE   **TACLOBAN**

ABUYOG

MANADUE   CAMOTES
SEA

CEBU

NEGROS

PANGLAO I.

TANJAY

DUMAGUETE

BOHOL

TAGBILARAN

BOHOL SEA

CAMIGUIN I.

SIARGAO I.

SURIGAO

PUERTO PRINCESA

PALAWAN

QUEZON

ILIGAN
BAY

DIPOLOG

OZAMIS   ILIGAN

MARAWI

CAGAYAN DE ORO

TUBBATAHA
REEFS

BROOKE'S POINT

SULU

SEA

ILLANA
BAY

COTABATO   **DAVAO**

SAMAL I.

MINDANAO

ZAMBOANGA

ISABELA   LAMITAN

MORO
GULF

LAKE SEBU   DAVAO
GULF

**GENERAL
SANTOS
CITY**

BASILAN ISLAND

JOLO   JOLO

TAWI TAWI

CELEBES SEA

Acknowledgements

A most heartfelt thanks to the Corporate and Individual Sponsors. Thank you for believing in me and this project before a single page was printed, and for helping make this dream book a reality.

Special thanks to Secretary Gemma Cruz-Araneta of the Philippine Department of Tourism, and to Commissioner General Mina T. Gabor, World Expo 2002 Philippines.

My deepest thanks to Former President Corazon Aquino, Mr. Nick Joaquin, and Don Jaime Zobel de Ayala for writing your words for this book; to Jose Campos Jr, Liz Chase, Ambassador Howard Dee, Mrs. Betty Dee, Richard Dee, Susana del Mundo, Mr. Carlos C. Ejercito, and Dann Ilicic—this book may not exist today without your moral support, encouragement and assistance.

Many, many thanks to the fine establishments that extended their generous hospitality during the shoots:

Alavar Seafoods House
Apo View Hotel
Ardent Hot Springs Resort
Asia World Resort Hotel
Balaw-Balaw Restaurant
Banaue Hotel & Youth Hostel
Bohol Beach Club
Dusit Hotel Nikko
EDSA Plaza Hotel (Shangri-La)
El Nido Resorts

Fort Ilocandia Resort Hotel
Hidden Valley Springs
Insular Century Hotel Davao
Lantaka Hotel
Leyte Park Hotel
Manila Galleria Suites
Manila Hotel
Mar y Cielo Resort
Marawi Resort Hotel
Mayon International Hotel

Pagsanjan Rapids Hotel
Park Place Hotel
Pearl Farm Beach Resort
Phela Grande Hotel
Plantation Bay Mactan
Pryce Plaza Hotel
Shangri-La Hotel Manila
Traders Hotel
Villa Escudero

Maraming salamat to the hundreds of individuals, companies and establishments who extended their hospitality and assistance or otherwise made this journey more enjoyable and rewarding. Apologies to those who have been inadvertently omitted due to a failing memory and lost records.

Cecilia
Doy
Gilly
Lizillyn
Nimfa
Oca
Mang Tony
Mila A. Abad
Fernando Abay
Annette D. Africano
Catherine Madrid Agregado
Editha C. Alano
Teresa V. Alejandrino
Rachel Alejandro
Marissa A. Alfaro
Mr. & Mrs. Alindogan
Hon. Bryan M. Aliping
Helen Amadeo Angderson
Jay Angeles
Karen Anson
Angie Anthony
Angel Aquino
Luchi P. Asuncion
Issa Austria
Mel R. Barbon
Rey C. Bascon
Theresa Joy Bete
Rosalie E. Blume
Bonjin N. Bolinao
Freddy Borromeo
Fe Burog
Anna Cadiz
Tess Campillo
Butch & Ollie Campos
Elizabeth Campos
Jay Campos
Jeffrey Campos
Jose & Beatrice Campos
Evangeline B. Cappleman
Gener Carlos
Armi Caunan
Christine Faron Chan
Liz Chase
Walter & Jan G. Cheng
John & Harvey Chua
Robert Chulsi
Kim Concepcion
Michelle Concepcion
Vince Cordero
Daniel Corpuz
Arlene Z. Couderc
Isabelo Crisostomo
Andres Cristobal Cruz
Elison M. Cuesta
Jesselle Marie T. Cui
Amparo Dacudao-Buncad

Catalina S. Dakudao
Pinky David
Julie Yap Daza
Sylvia de Castro
Felix R. de los Santos
Danding & Tang De Villa
Didi Dee
Marybeth Dee
Odette Dee
Richard & Viel Dee
Simeon & Marietta Dee
Gunther Deichmann
Ana Carla Dela Paz
Sohura Dimaampao
Resty E. Dimacuha
Wilfred A. Diu
Mike C. Domingo
Atty. Macario Duguiang
Rodolfo Eco Dula
Ethel Echevarria
Charrie Elinzano
Conrado Escudero
Bebot Estillore
Icelle Borja Estrada
Gemma Estrella
Bonge Fabian
Leny Roco Fabul
Menchie Fajardo
Ric Favis
Donna Kristine Faylona
Mona Lisa Felipe
Catherine Joy Fernan
Ramon & Barbara Flores
Victor A. Francisco
Romeo M. Gacad
Gov. Antonio Gallardo
Martin Galvez
Garch Garchitorena
Mayor Alvin & Ninette Garcia
Roy Garcia
Tetet Z. Geroy
Sander Gilles
Ferdie N. Gilles
Serafin Gonzales
Josie & Jess Gonzalez
Kevin Gosinco
Isagani G. Granali
Aleli Guevarra
Ruffa Gutierrez
Dr. & Mrs. Carlos Guzman
Mike Guzman
Patrick Guzman
Kevin Hamdorf
Iain Hamilton
Jocelyn Hess
Pilar A. Hilario

Jose Mari H. Hilario
Doris Ho
Craig Holm
Eduviges Y. Huang
Dr. Genevieve Huang
Johnie U. Icotanim
Liza Ilarde
Roque & Erlinda Juatco
Suzie Ketene
Jacinto & Glory Ko
Cindy B. Lapid
Mary Latorre
Daisy Lemay
Suzanne Lemay
Bill P. Lewis
Joan R. Lewis
Gari P. Lim
Benjie C. Lopez
Cristina Lopez
Alfie Lorenzo
Jenny C. Luna
Shaira Luna
Fred Maciado
Marirose B. Maneru
Delta Martin Bernardo
Albert Martinez
Chie Martinez
Evelyn Mayuga
Greg McKinnon
Joey Mead
Sym Mendoza
Mercy Melchor
Jon Miller
Dr. Ariel Miranda
Nemi R. Miranda
France Misa
Carmelita Mondiguing
Febs D. Mondonedo
Jing Monis
Norma M. Morantte
Regina Munoz
Barbara J. Murray
Andy Naval
Andre Naval
Dr. Carlos G. Naval
Dr. Sullian Naval
June & Zeny Naval
Marcel & Rosalie Naval
Marvi Naval
Marvi & Marilou Naval
Peps Naval
Mandy Navasero
Leona Nepumoceno
Nicholas Neri
Fernando Ocampo
Jonathan Ong

Alex L. Orbito
Daryl Orchard
Sari Ortega
Monina Ouano
Dorothy Jean Pabayo
Catherine V. Pascual
Peachy Pelaez
Glenn Peralta
Maritess Perez
Jobee & Tata Pineda
Roland & Ping Pineda
Patrick A. Popek
Jose & Isabel Puyat
Lita Puyat
Jenelyn F. Ramos
Mayor Arturo Regalado
Rejie Regalado
Elizabeth V. Reyes
Marita Reyes
Dino Ricafort
Eli Ricafort
Peping & Zon Ricafort
Annie D. Ringor
Marciel Q. Rios
Francis M. Rivera
Jing Rivera
Patria Aurora Roa
Rosanna R. Roman
Mike & Menchita Romulo
Anna Melissa L. Rosario
Marcelo Rubinos
Ricky Sajise
Susan Salcedo
Onching U. Salinel
Nory Samson
Marge San Jose
Ricardo A. San Juan
Sherylle C. Santarin
Evita T. Sarenas
Eric & Tess Severino
Leahlizbeth A. Sia
Erwin & Frances Siao
Jing Sipin
George Sison
Bing Sitoy
Robert Siy
Karen Somerville
Rudolf Studer
Walter P. Sultan
Aya Sunga
Ignacio Sunico
Allen Arvin Tan
Danny Tan
Dorothy S. Tan
Lory Tan
Marlinda Angbetic Tan

Philip Tan
Sukarno D. Tanggol
John A. Tanjanco
Raul J. Teehankee
Sonny R. Teves
Pamela C. Tiu
Mel Tobias
Malou S. Torres
Edwin Trompeta
Nonong S. Tumada
Edwin Tuyay
Wig Tysmans
Elizabeth Uy
Patrick Uy
Richard Uy
Ines Valdez-Silvestre
Lisa Villamor
Amor Villegas
Benet Vital
Perdigon Vocalan
Timothy & Pinky Yang
Angeli Yap
Sari Yap
Salvador Yee Loy
Gigi M. Zulueta, Jr.

Adphoto
Crucible Gallery
Euphoria
Finale Art Galery
Holiday Inn Manila Pavilion
Lifestyle Asia
Manila Cathedral
Manila Peninsula Hotel
Manila Polo Club
Marquee
MEGA Magazine
National Bookstore
Nayong Pilipino
Nemiranda Arthouse
Pearl Farm
Philippine Airlines
PCVC
Philippine Tourism
Authority
Ricafort Farm
Westin Philippine Plaza
Zu

Sponsors

Corporate Sponsors:

United Laboratories

E.B. EDDY PAPER

Individual Sponsors:

Mr. & Mrs. Arthur Ang

Ambassador Howard Dee and Mrs. Betty Dee

Mr. Stanley Dee

Mr. Greg Dumas

Mr. Steve Good

Mr. Manny Gonzalez
Plantation Bay Resort

Mr. Richard A. Gray, Jr.

Mrs. Josie Cruz Natori

Dr. Rey D. Pagtakhan, M.P.
Parliamentary Secretary to the Prime Minister of Canada

Mr. Mark V. Pangilinan

Mr. Johnny Valdes
Johnny Air Cargo

Atty. James Wolf

Ms. Mona Lisa Yuchengco
Publisher, Filipinas Magazine

About the Photographer

STUART NAVAL DEE was born in the Philippines and immigrated to Canada in 1973. He studied painting and photography and graduated from the University of British Columbia with a Bachelor of Fine Arts degree.

Based in Vancouver, he has photographed extensively in over thirty countries throughout Europe, Asia and the Americas, dividing his time between fine art, magazine, and advertising work. His images have been published worldwide. The first book featuring his photography exclusively was APA Publications' *Insight Guide to Vancouver*, published in 1993. That same year, he was chosen as one of seven international photographers to photograph Slovenia for a traveling exhibit on the new country. The following year, he was selected as one of ten photographers to shoot *Philippines, A Spirit of Place*, for the Philippine Department of Tourism. His work was also included in Kodak's *10,000 Eyes*, the book commemorating the 150th anniversary of photography. In between other assignments over the last five years, he has returned repeatedly to the Philippines to create this book. When his travel schedule allows, he also teaches workshops on vision, color, and travel photography.

Technical Notes

All photographs are by Stuart Dee, taken with Canon cameras and lenses. Cameras: A2E, EOS-1N; Lenses: 17-35/2.8, 20-35/2.8, 50/1.8, 70-210/4.5, 70-200/2.8, 1.4x converter. Underwater photographs were taken with a Canon A1 (except for page 109, photo by Bob Yin).

All photographs were taken on Fujichrome film and processed at Customcolor Photo Lab in Vancouver. Films: Velvia, Provia, Sensia, RDP100, Fujichrome 400.

For additional copies of this book, please check at your local bookstore. If not available, or for quantity discounts, please visit the website at www.studeeo.com/book, or email odyssey@studeeo.com.